I am the Face of Hope

I made it

to tell the story.

VANESSA B. CARTER

Published by the author

© Copyright 2022 by Vanessa B. Carter

All rights reserved. This book, or any parts thereof, may not be reproduced in any form or by any means without the expressed permission in writing from the publisher.

I Am the Face of Hope

Published by Vanessa B. Carter

ISPB: 979-8-9856646-0-7

Printed in the United States of America

Scripture quotations marked CEV are taken from the Holy Bible, Contemporary English Version ®. Copyright ©1995 American Bible Society. All rights reserved.

Scripture quotations marked ESV are taken from the Holy Bible, English Standard Version®. Copyright ©2001 by Crossway, a publishing ministry of Good News Publishers. All rights reserved.

Scripture quotations marked NKJV are taken from The Holy Bible. New King James Version®. Copyright © by Thomas Nelson. Used by permission. All rights reserved.

Scripture quotations marked NLT are taken from The Holy Bible, New Living Translation ®. Copyright ©1996, 2004, 2007, 2013 by Tyndale House Foundation. Used by permission of Tyndale House Publishers Inc., Carol Stream, Illinois 60188. All rights reserved.

Please note that the author chooses to capitalize pronouns in scripture that refer to the Father, Son and Holy Spirit. This may differ from the bible publisher's format.

Eds. Quantina Jackson, Jasmine Robinson, and Leah Segar

Cover and interior design by Medina Isiah Designs
(www.design.medinaisiah.com)

Cover photo by Keith King of Revolution Images and Media
(www.revolution-images.com)

I dedicate this book to my birth mother, E. Delores Bowers, who is the reason for living my life. I dedicate this book to my parents, Lorenzo and Louise Johnson, who raised and instilled Christian values in me, and I dedicate this book to my son, Larry B. Jones, Jr. who made me a mommy. These are my angels who look over me every day of my life.

I dedicate this book to those who have had losses in their lives and think there is no way to get through the darkness. I dedicate this book to those who have experienced mental and/or physical and sexual abuse. You are not to blame, and don't allow yourself to be tormented by the pain.

Know that God is right there with you, and you can heal and live the rest of your life in peace. You may feel like you are alone, but you are not. It is important to reach out to those who love you. Reach out to a therapist and/or a psychiatrist because these are tools God has had created for those who are hurting.

When you commit yourself to healing, it will take place. Be kind to yourselves and take one day at a time. Be open to new opportunities that may come your way or create an opportunity. Be a presence for someone who needs the care and love you can give.

I dedicate this book to those who have gotten stuck in their pain. To let them know, *"Weeping may endure for a night, But joy comes in the morning." – (Psalm 30:5 (NKJV)*

Table of Contents

Acknowledgements i

Foreword iii

Introduction v

Arise 1

The Babe, the Child, and Her Protectors 11

The Teenager, Adventures and Safe Haven 19

A Priceless Gift 25

The Mother 29

The Motherless 35

A New Life 45

The Visionary 49

The Deliverance 55

Higher Ground 67

Totally Available 71

Acknowledgements

First and foremost, I thank God for being my rock. I thank Him for never letting go of my hand. I thank Him for allowing me to tell my story. I give all praises, glory and honor to Him.

Next, I want to thank my husband for always being a support. Even when he doesn't understand why I do what I do. I am always reminded that he is my covering. I love you, Michael Carter. Thanks for loving me.

I thank my Carter tribe for welcoming me into the family and loving me with all my craziness. Your welcoming arms have been lifesaving. Thank you for how you love me. I love you so very much.

I would like to thank my bonus son, Mikey, for allowing me to love on him and my grandson, Angel, who is my heartthrob. I also thank God for all my Godchildren: Sherri Goodine, Marie Hayes, Carl Brown, Xavier Creekmur, Keith King and Curtis Hutchinson. I love you ever so much.

I would like to thank my aunt, Denise Mason, and my cousins, Nicole Mason and Jacqueline Hobbs. They have been so instrumental in always encouraging me. I love you to the moon and back.

I would like to thank my dear friend Bessie Smith for being my sounding board and praying me through anything that troubles me. I thank her for sharing her boys with me and making sure I get her delicious cabbage and fruitcake. I love you, My Bessie.

I would love to thank all my friends who love me, correct me, pray for me, laugh at and with me, and sing with me. You know who you are, and God chose each of you to be in my life. I love you ever so much.

I thank God for the Board of Directors of The Delores Foundation. Our Past Vice President, Medina Isiah, Angela Nelson, Carol Davis, Jennifer Rivers, and Kristina Williams. You stick by my side as you bring expertise to our foundation. You are movers and shakers, and I am glad to have you as my teammates. I would also like to thank Medina Isiah for pouring into the foundation and opening doors for us. Ladies, I love you so very much.

I would like to thank my friend, Pastor Teresa, who poured into me what I needed to move this book forward. I love you Sis.

I would like to thank the readers in the hope that you will find this book to be encouraging.

Foreword

We all encounter thousands upon thousands of people in our lifetime, but has there ever been one endearing person you're automatically drawn to no matter what season you're in? Their smile lures you into a world forgetting the concerns of your own, an energetic spirit that lifts yours, and words unforgettable, 'Good morning Ms. Marie, about that awesome cake. May I place my order? Thank you ma'am.' Yes. That was November, 2017 when I was able to get to know Vanessa very quickly as a mother figure in my life. Her words were sweet, direct and to the point which I loved and began calling her 'Mama V'. Before we connected, she experienced her aneurysm in 2015, but at this moment in the spring of 2018, she shared with me her full story right there in my backyard. I saw her humble heart and unapologetic gratefulness towards God for bringing her through.

Vanessa's love for plants is amazing. She could specifically identify each plant by its horticultural name. I watched her maneuver through Home Depot knowing which type of plants worked well with others. That's when it hit me deeply, and I understood why God connected us. She reminded me so much of the mother I lost years ago, but God was orchestrating time events in His own way. He knew I needed Vanessa to step in and help me grow into a better woman. She's tough and has had her moments of disparities, as many of us, but I have always been so proud to witness her bounce backs, victories, strength, endurance and her empowerment for other women given unselfishly. She was no longer Vanessa or Mama V, she was my Mother...Mama. My inspiration. My she-ro. My life. God purposed her for me. Now there's no secret to her as my Mama, I give side-eye emoji looks with question marks towards other women who try to call her the same. "Mmmm, we don't do that here." But I get it and it's understood why. Her core...her spirit...radiates and it's magnetic, like a moth to a flame. Every woman needs a Vanessa. A Mother of Hope to all.

I am honored to express the love on paper for an amazing woman of God. I am touched by the many women she has inspired through the years, the giving of blankets and food to the homeless, The Delores Foundation named after her own mother, Candlelight Memorial Services in remembrance of lost loved ones, a grief counselor, an ordained minister, and absolutely a great friend to all. Yet I am touched and moved, but also enthused with anticipation for those yet to come to gather amongst the table with her and speak in words of encouragement. What a pleasure! Most of all, I am humble to be called 'Daughter' spoken through the lips of a woman who gives from the heart and stands with the face of Hope. I pray this book, "I Am the Face of Hope", inspires, motivates, encourages, and revitalizes your spirit to keep moving forward. As quoted from her book, "God prepared me for this journey…", life takes you on a journey, but God has equipped you along the way. You may not be able to see it upfront, but here's the remainder of her quote… "He provided me with a Word that would carry me through." Whatever God lays in your spirit, may the words from these pages penetrate it deeply for the next to see you as their face of hope.

~Roberta Marie Haye

Introduction

Amid some of the most painful experiences life will send our way, there is nothing we will encounter that God will not see us through. Even when we are not aware of His presence, He is near. He will cover us with His love and will always be that protecting force in our lives.

When we think that we cannot bare another painful experience is when God is at His best work in us, even though we don't recognize what He is doing. Our experiences are not meant to destroy us, but there is a powerful blessing on the other side if we do not give up. It is a call to lean and depend on God's grace, mercy, forgiveness, and most importantly, His Love.

What I am about to share is the calling the Lord placed on my life even before I was born. Sharing these events are powerful testimonies of God's power. I have lived through so much, but the "much" was not designed to destroy me, but to make me into who I am today and who God desires me to be for tomorrow.

"And let us not grow weary while doing good, for in due season we shall reap if we do not lose heart" – Galatians 6:9 (NKJV)

Many people have come into my life and have made such an indelible impression on my heart. I have taken what they have given, whether good or bad, and became the person that I am today.

My prayer is for whomever reads this book will find peace and comfort in who God says they are. That they may walk in the light of God's Glory with all of what He has given them.

When I look back, I can give more of me as God instructs. My past does not define me but propels me to move in my today as God prepares my tomorrows. God had a plan put into place and the events of my life whether I made the wrong turn or not. They have led me to finally be on the course He has created.

It was necessary for me to experience painful moments in my life. I am stronger and have been delivered from the chains, and am now released to have an outstretched hand. With the presence of the Holy Spirit, I can now help pull someone else through to their victory. This is all because of the Amazing Grace of God. Friends, this is my story.

"The Lord is good to those who depend on him, to those who search for him. So it is good to wait quietly for salvation from the LORD." - Lamentations 3:25-26 (NLT)

Chapter 1

Arise

On Saturday, April 11, 2015, my life began anew; it started with me preparing to lead a grief support group. I woke up with a slight headache, which was not unusual. Going through my day with a headache had become a way of life for me, so as usual, I took pain medication and continued with my morning.

When I arrived at Swansboro Baptist Church to lead 'A Safe Place' grief support group, I greeted the attendees and soon dismissed myself to the chapel for prayer and preparation. The attendees began to arrive, and once they were settled, I opened with a bit of dialogue followed by prayer. After the prayer, a severe pain shot through the right side of my temple, paralyzing me for a moment. The pain was excruciating and lasted for about ten minutes, leaving me with a dull headache.

I tried as best I could to get myself together, but it was difficult. I shared with the group what I had experienced and asked for just a moment to take more medication with a cup of hot tea. Once we reconvened, I did my best to focus, but that nagging headache became the center of my attention.

Our agenda was together in a circle of love where we would share whatever grief we may be experiencing. But instead, we were asked to participate in a mindfulness exercise. During this exercise, we had the option of closing our eyes and focusing on a calming place or keeping our eyes open, finding something on which to focus. As I closed my eyes, we were instructed to speak about peace to a painful part of our bodies; I focused on my pounding headache.

After this exercise, we created our circle. I opened this part of the support group with a song near and dear to my heart, 'His Presence Is Here to Heal.' I tried to focus on the words of the song, but I could not ignore the pounding in my head. Then, I noticed my right hand was beginning to feel numb; this caused me some concern, but not enough to abort my assignment with the group. However, thoughts were going through my mind about whether I should admit myself into a neighboring hospital, ask one of the attendees to take me home or call my husband to come and pick me up. Of course, I opted to drive myself home. I did call home to share with my husband how I was feeling, and when I arrived at the house, there he stood waiting for me in our driveway.

As I turned into my driveway, I noticed a young lady and her baby approaching me. I was not in the mood to entertain anyone, but I could not turn her away. She was an incredibly special person in our lives who we had not seen in years, and this would be our first time meeting her son. So, we all journeyed into the house together. First, my husband checked my blood pressure, which was normal. So, once again, I took pain medication in hopes that it would provide me a measure of relief from the pain. Then, I commenced playing with the baby. At the end of our visit, the young lady's mother picked her up, and to my surprise, we became acquainted with her. Another conversation ensued, after which I retreated to my bedroom to rest and prayerfully sleep my headache off.

Unfortunately for me, however, this period of relaxation was short-lived because we had a birthday luncheon invitation. This gathering was for our niece, so I had to attend it. Once again, I endured the pain of my headache to show up for my family, and once again, our visit was short-lived because I could not relieve myself of this pounding headache.

As soon as we got home, I immediately retreated to the bedroom and stretched out for a couple of hours of rest, after which I proceeded to wash my hair and spend time in my office preparing a sermon for the next day. Although my head was throbbing on both sides, I could not stop because I had not finished my assignment for the church. Besides, how dare I contact this Pastor – who was counting on me – to inform him that I would not be able to bring forth the Word of God. I could not abort this assignment, so I continued to forge ahead.

It was now early Sunday morning, and I was not feeling any better, so though I moved slowly, I continued purposefully as I prepared for the day. My Aunt and I journeyed to the other side of the city to a church we had never attended. The service layout was quite different from what we were accustomed to. The service was scheduled to begin at 11:00 am, but with it being a multicultural atmosphere, the preliminaries were extended. It was not until 1:00 pm that I delivered my message; I was feeling horrible by this time.

The sermon was titled "A Closer Walk" - Proverbs 3:5-6 from the NKJV reads: "Trust in the Lord with all your heart and lean not on your understanding; In all your ways acknowledge him, and he shall direct your path."

The words from the sermon fed me: "There is a familiar ole hymn that comes to mind. Just a closer walk with Thee, Grant it, Jesus, is my plea; Daily walking close to Thee, let it be, dear Lord, let it be."

As a loving father, God gives words to guide His children through life's difficulties, temptations, and dilemmas. When we, as His children, listen to His voice and seek His wisdom, He will show us the right way to go in every situation. God prepared me for this journey and gave me a word to carry me through.

My Aunt Denise—who has always been my "ride or die"— had accompanied me, and she kept a close eye on me the entire day. She could tell I was not 100%, so she continued praying for me as we headed back home. Once we had settled in at home, my intentions to bless my aunt for her graciousness and support revealed much more than expected. I presented her with a love offering as a check, and she became keenly aware that something was not right when she noticed how my penmanship had taken a turn for the worst. I did not recognize my handwriting until then, but I felt as if I had lost control of any ability to correct it. At this point, I am feeling increasingly concerned.

My headache continued to plague me, and nothing I did, no amount of medication, and no amount of rest caused it to subside. Finally, my husband checked on me and asked if I needed to visit the hospital, and I declined. However, I figured I needed to try an alternative remedy at this point, so I asked my husband if he would purchase BC powder since the Excedrin Migraine was not working. It was as if the pain in my head laughed whenever it encountered what I would consider relief.

As Sunday evening ended, I finally drifted off to sleep ever so briefly. To my annoyance and distress, I woke up with that same pain in my head. As I began my workday on Monday, April 13, 2021, I realized my penmanship was still off. I took the first call and realized my speech was garbled. Something was wrong, and it was now causing considerable concern. So, I contacted my primary care physician's office. I shared with the administrative assistant the course of events. She informed me that the physician was not in and that I could make an appointment later that week. Her response floored me. I am confident she could hear that my speech was impaired. So, I informed my supervisor of my condition and apologized for having to leave.

I notified my husband of my desire to come home and was taken to the emergency room. He graciously took me to my hospital of choice – Henrico Doctors Hospital on Skipwith Road in Richmond, VA. There was only one patient ahead of us, so the wait was approximately 15 minutes.

Once I spoke with the attending physician and shared my symptoms, he immediately ordered various tests. I had to undergo an MRI, a CAT scan, and an MRA. After a series of tests, the emergency room physician referred me to a Neurosurgeon, and I was admitted to the hospital, which shocked me. What was going on here? I came in thinking I was given medication for migraines, and now I have doctors poking and prodding me. I was desperate for answers, and boy did I get one. When I met with the Neurosurgeon, I learned that I had suffered a cerebral aneurysm and had an AVM next to it. I was in enough shock hearing that I had suffered an aneurysm. I could not at that moment wrap my head around what it meant to have an AVM next to it. What was this doctor saying to me?

So next, the doctor begins to explain that an aneurysm is a blood clot in the brain. In my case, this blood clot was in the cerebellum, the portion of my brain that controls my balance. I was told I had a brain bleed sufficient to fill a thimble, and then the bleeding stopped. WOW! The tests also revealed the AVM (Arteriovenous Malformation).

An AVM is an abnormal connection between arteries and veins, preventing blood from properly flowing through my capillary system. It is these capillaries that play a significant role in circulation. They deliver oxygen in the blood to the tissues in the body and facilitate the transport of nutrients in the body. So, not only did I bleed in my brain, but the nutrients in the blood that feed other parts of my body were not being delivered because the vehicle meant to transport them was damaged.

The AVM disorder had been with me from birth, but without the advent of the aneurysm, it may have gone untreated and caused irreparable damage to my health in later years. But God! What was so remarkable about this phenomenon is that about 1% of people suffer from it, and most have no idea.

I was admitted into the hospital immediately, and the remaining tests were conducted once in my room. On the following day, April 14th, I was taken by ambulance to Johnston-Willis Hospital, where I would undergo further tests and treatment.

My room was full of a constant flow of doctors, nurses, and administrators. Then one lady came over to me and whispered in my ear that I was in God's care and everything would be all right. I was not allowed to use the bathroom alone, so we all knew what was next, THE BED PAN!

Everything was happening so quickly. The next thing I knew, in came the ambulance attendees who so caringly placed me on a gurney, and off I went. This ordeal surprised me because I was neither nervous nor afraid. In all honesty, I was SHOCKED, but at peace!

Once I arrived at Johnston Willis Hospital, they moved me to the ICU (Intensive Care Unit). There was a team of nurses waiting for me when I arrived. Right away, they bathed me and prepared me for an angiogram. It was an eye-closing experience to have a nurse on either side of me as I lay in the nude. So, I did just that—I closed my eyes while they did their job. WHEW!

On April 14th, I was transported by ambulance from Henrico Doctors to Johnston - Willis hospital to undergo further tests and treatment for AVM. While at Johnston-Willis, my room was filled with doctors, nurses, and administrators. I felt so vulnerable and oppressed. During one of my weakest moments, a nurse attendant whispered, "you are in God's care," gently in my ear. At that moment, I knew that God was with me.

As for the angiogram, this was something I had only heard about, but now I was getting to experience it firsthand. I could not for the life of me wrap my head around the physicians looking at my brain through my groin. Yes, I said they had to go through my groin to get an x-ray of my brain. Praise God for sedation and local anesthesia.

As the nurses came in and out of my room, they provided me with the utmost care. They possessed beautiful spirits and the most beautiful and pleasant presence. They became family as they took care of me. We comforted each other by sharing personal stories of trials and triumphs, which was a blessing.

Once my surgeon came to share the prognosis and the plan of action, I must admit I became a little shaken as I had the opportunity to get a look at my brain on the x-ray. Wow, what an adventure. But I could find comfort in the fact that my husband was always by my side. Our son, my traveling aunt, and dear friend were daily visitors. I did not have to travel this road alone. THANK GOD!

It was now time for me to transition from ICU to the Neurological floor since a room was available. I finally understood why I was in the ICU first; it was because a room had to become available on the floor. My physician was determined not to release me but to place me nearby. What an insightful physician. He knew the danger I was in, even though I did not.

On Thursday, April 16th, I was moved to the Neurology floor, where I met more lovely nursing staff who wowed me with their presence. My visitations increased in size and frequency. My grandbabies came to share time with me, as well as sharing my hospital bed on the days they visited. It was all a great adventure for them. More calls, cards, and gifts poured in, which indeed showed me how much I was loved.

My grandson's teacher allowed him to make me a special card in class. In it, he shared how they prayed for me and wanted me to get well soon: but what jumped out at me was, and I quote, "We made the devil run. Now that said it all. With all the visitors coming and going, my heart was warm and full of joy. However, I found it to be quite emotional when the time came for my husband to leave. I knew this was the time I needed to move closer to God and allow His comfort to fill me. After a brief cry, I focused on God's goodness.

When the traffic of loved ones concluded and my husband was no longer there to give me strength, I had to turn to the scriptures for comfort. "Trust in the Lord with all your heart and lean not on your understanding. In all your ways, acknowledge Him, and He shall direct your path." - Proverbs 3:5-6 (NKJV). These words kept me, fed me, and infused me with God's love during this season of my life. These words gave me life, liberty, and a reason to continue this journey—to be a better Christian and servant of God.

It is Monday, April 20th, and the time has come for me to have the aneurysm coiling—which would stop the blood flow into the aneurysm. While waiting in the holding area with my husband and aunt, a nurse came to inform me there was a visitor who wanted to come back. My question was, "who is this person?"

When asked who she was, the only response was that it was the church's lady. My husband went to check for me, and low and behold, it was my dear friend. Not only a dear friend but also a prayer warrior who, for whatever reason, did not give her name. What a relief. Recognizing that it was her, not some strange intruder, she gave all of us a laugh and took the edge off.

On April 20th, I was preparing to have a coiling procedure for my aneurysm when my friend surprised me and joined my husband and aunt at the hospital.

My neurosurgeons and interns came in for me to sign the proper documents, and then my anesthesiologist informed me of his procedure. He commented openly on my big smile and pretty teeth and said that he rarely saw this. I thought that was kind of him. All I wanted to ensure was that I would be provided with the patch to prevent me from getting sick from the anesthesia. He assured me I would have one. That alone made him my friend.

While discussing my procedure, the anesthesiologist was very friendly and personable. He put me at ease after complimenting my smile and explaining how I would be given a patch to prevent me from becoming ill after the anesthesia.

The time came for the procedure, and my three angels, my husband, aunt, and friend, kissed me and said they would see me later. I went into the Angiogram room and was put to sleep. Of course, it did not seem long to me, but before you knew it, I was in recovery, taken care of once again by a beautiful nurse.

One of my neurosurgeons came in to see how I was doing and reported that everything went well. He wrote to my husband and family as well. I returned to the ICU, where I was monitored for 24 hours. I was highly impressed with my nurse's level of care after my procedure. Before his shift ended, I learned that he was not just a nurse but a pastor.

I received wise counsel from him, which stayed with me and educated me on the seriousness of what I had endured. I now have a responsibility to share with others the importance of heeding the warning signs. Our bodies will speak to us when something is out of order; we need to listen and act. I was blessed because he allowed me to live to tell the tale. PRAISE GOD!!!!

Well, it is Tuesday, April 21st, and I am preparing to go home. WOW! This was a fantastic journey, and God heard my prayer because I did not want to be in the hospital on my birthday, April 24th. Thank you, Lord.

It was time to be discharged. I got myself dressed and waited patiently for my release instructions. As the nurse wheeled me through the hospital corridors, I breathed a sigh of relief. As the nurse assisted me into my car, it looked good; the trees looked good; the grass looked good; the pavement looked good, and other vehicles looked good. Once we hit the interstate, the signs looked good; paying the toll was good; everything I witnessed looked much better than I remembered.

This was all because of L-I-F-E. God had given me another opportunity, and I am eternally grateful. I did not fear because He was with me every step of the way. What I have experienced are healing and restoration. I am feeling great and could not wait to see and smell my home.

As we pulled into the driveway, tears began to fill my eyes because I had a new lease on life. Home is still home as it stands, but a different me enters. What a mighty God we serve; angels bow before Him; heaven and earth adore Him. What a powerful God we serve!

Now I am on the road to recovery and rejuvenation, which was humbling. I continued to give God all the praise and glory for how he manifested himself during this time. Oh, this was not all because I still have the AVM, which needs to be taken care of later.

I prayed not to be in the hospital on my birthday, and God granted me that prayer. On April 24th, I celebrated my 63rd birthday like never. I have been blessed with the gift of L-I-F-E and the opportunity to reflect on this life.

On May 8th, I returned to work and was showered with an abundance of love. I now know it was not all about me but about the persons whose lives had also been changed. I was not driving yet, so I had a limousine service that provided me with all my transportation needs, and I was so grateful to them. The days and weeks passed as God prepared me for procedure number two.

In June of the same year, I entered the Neurosurgical Unit in the same hospital for the Gamma Knife Procedure, a form of radiation used to treat brain disorders. This procedure did not involve a surgical incision into the brain despite its name. Also, the "blades" of the gamma "knife" were beams of highly focused gamma-ray radiation.

Up to 192 beams of radiation are precisely focused on the targeted area in the brain. Because the beams are so highly focused, there was slight damage to the surrounding healthy tissue. The place to be treated was carefully identified with neuroimaging before the gamma knife radiosurgery, also known as stereotactic radiation, was used to treat brain disorders.

To prepare me for the procedure, I had the same anesthesiologist for the aneurysm coiling. Nothing but God's hand at work. Thank you, Lord, for your favor in my life. Now this man sees quite a few patients, so how did he recognize me? It was my God-given smile he remembered.

There were connectors feeding radiation into my brain to burn off the AVM, which could take two and a half years to disappear. I listened to jazz while the procedure was taking place. I was calm. This was nothing but God's peace that was with me.

Every six months, I had to have an MRI and MRA to check on the status of the AVM. It was completely gone within one year. The last visit to the neurosurgeon was in June of 2019, and he released me to see him in ten years. THANK YOU, GOD!

All Glory, Honor, and Praise I give to God. He walked with me all the way and allowed me to achieve what I could never have done alone. As I look back over these life-altering events, I am reminded of how awesome of a God we serve. He allowed me to live to tell the story, so as you read, know there is a purpose in all of what I have encountered.

This journey of my life allowed me to look back and realize how important it is to capture the essence of life. I now share with you my life story as it unfolds the essence of who I was and who I am.

Chapter 2

The Babe, the Child, and Her Protectors

I was born on Thursday, April 24, 1952, to E. Delores Bowers, who was told I had severe meningitis. The doctors instructed her to wait twenty-four hours to name me. Twenty-four hours passed, and here it was – April 25th, and all was well. She called her little bundle of joy, Vanessa Patricia Bowers.

"For you formed my inward parts; you knitted me together in my mother's womb. I praise you, for I am fearfully and wonderfully made. Wonderful are your works; my soul knows it very well." - Psalm 139:13-14 (ESV)

On July 18, 1953, at the tender age of fifteen months, my life drastically changed. My 21-year-old working mother felt like it was time to have some fun. She and her friends decided to take a trip to the boardwalk of Atlantic City, but she needed someone to keep me.

A friend of my mother who was visiting from Richmond agreed to keep me at the last minute. Had it not been for the visiting friend, my mother would not have gone or would have taken me. There was much to take into consideration, yet there was much unknown.

My mom and her friends made their journey, but what was meant to be a day trip turned into a nightmare. During their drive back, the driver fell asleep behind the wheel on the New Jersey Turnpike. He ran into a telegraph pole, and all the passengers were killed except the driver. My mother was thrown from the car and died instantly.

After the unexpected passing of my mother, my great uncles traveled to New Jersey by train to relocate me back to Richmond, Virginia, to the neighborhood of Washington Park, on the North Side of Richmond. I have often wondered about that trip. Two men and a fifteen-month-old little girl on a train from New Jersey.

The Babe, the Child, and Her Protectors

One of my great uncles and my great aunt were the ones with the task of rearing me. Since they were the only parents I had, they became my mommy and daddy. Not only did they have the task of raising me, but they had also raised my mother. I could only imagine what they must have been feeling. Note, this was in the 1950s, and family took care of family, and these two have taken many in, and I was another boarder—a little one.

As a little girl around five years old, I remember talking to a white Dutch chair as if my birth mother were sitting there. Those conversations were so comforting; I remember them as if they were yesterday. These encounters gave me a sense of belonging, but they disturbed my mommy terribly. She became so uncomfortable that she moved the chair outside by the trash pile. This was where they would burn trash on the weekends.

I was so distraught that I found my way to sitting on the ground near that chair but got caught, and she eventually burned the chair. I remained right there and returned day after day. I was chastised for that too. So, I climbed a Mimosa tree to continue my conversations where mommy could not see me.

I always knew something different about myself but did not know what it was. I was missing my birth mother and longing for her. This was my way of connecting to her spirit and feeling close to her. My mommy did not recognize this. This was the beginning of her abuse.

"Am I a God near at hand," says the LORD, "And not a God afar off?" - Jeremiah 23:23 (NKJV)

My great-grandmother, who lived with us, was my protector. Nanny, who was my great-grandmother, used a wheelchair. As a little girl, I was engaged in ballet lessons every Saturday. I remember one Saturday, I could not draw myself away from the cartoons to get ready, and mommy threw a handful of silverware at me to get my attention. To Nanny's lap, I ran. Her lap was that safe place.

When I began school, my first-grade teacher was the greatest person I knew. I will never forget her. Her name was Mrs. Arrington, and she treated me like I was her own. There were many weekends I spent with her family. The love and compassion she gave me showed God's love for me. She lived across the street from Armstrong High School, and her children and I would play on the school grounds. At that time, I did not know this was the school my birth mother attended. Even though it was in a different location, it was still the same school.

When I was seven years old, I remember walking home from school and seeing cars outside our house—more cars than usual. When I walked into the house, my mommy told me that Nanny had died. Oh, my goodness, what would I do without my Nanny?

I was left to fend for myself. Sitting in her wheelchair comforted me and made me feel safe until it was no longer there one day. It left a hole in my heart and an impossible level of fear.

At the age of eight, I began to take piano lessons and labored through lessons and hours of practice. Each day I was bound to practice for one hour except for Saturdays and Sundays when I was given a reprieve. I remember journeying around the corner every Wednesday to my music teacher's house for a solid hour unless there was a storm. If one brewed, there were no lessons, and I was set free. WHEW!

I loved soap opera music, and I played some of the theme songs by ear. My mommy would hear me and make me go outside and pick my switches off a tree. If they were too skinny, mommy would add to my few. I would view my whelps, feel sorry for myself, and then go back to practicing my lessons.

I was a curious child, and close to our piano was a round drum table full of brass figures. I looked in the drawer closest to me. I found a treasure: a newspaper article about my mother's car accident. In the article was a picture of the car, and it was hard to believe there were survivors because it was so mangled.

My mom's name in that article made it so real to me. This revelation was short-lived because I pulled the drawer open one day, and the article was gone. It was never to be seen again.

While growing up, mommy would often compare me to my birth mother. She informed me of how I did not measure up, which made me sad; this lessened my feeling of self-worth and lowered my self-esteem. Attending school was challenging because the other children would talk about their mommies and daddies; I could only dream of having either.

Sometimes if I did not clean the kitchen sink to my mommy's expectation, she would strike with whatever she could get in her hand. It could be an extension cord or a yardstick. Saturday morning was time to sleep late. On Saturday, while snoozing, I felt excruciating pain across my back. I was hit with a bamboo pole used to deliver dry-cleaned oriental rugs. I slept too late.

Why would an adult abuse a little child so badly? What would possess someone to hurt a helpless child? Reflecting on those years placed a yearning in my spirit to become an advocate for children in foster care.

When we as a family sat for meals, I was made to eat all my food no matter how long it took. I would hear stories of children who did not have food. That was supposed to make me feel sorry for them and grateful for my portion, but it did not. I still fought to eat what I did not like, so I ate it first and moved on to what tasted good. I tried it, and it sometimes worked, but not for every meal.

I sat at the table with cold scrambled eggs in front of me. I was eventually released from the table. There were times I hid those eggs under the table in the opening for the leaf and pretended that I had eaten them. The table, on occasion, needed to be enlarged with the leaf to seat more people. Once I was asked to set the table but open it first to insert the leaf, allowing more people to be seated at the table. I was at one end, and Denise was at the other end. We pulled the table apart, and there was an unrecognizable glob. It was eggs that I did not eat. After breakfast, I forgot to come back and remove them. No telling how long they were there.

God was with me through it all and provided safe havens for me. I paid visits and received love and attention elsewhere. These homes were full of laughter, as I had a way of escaping those unpleasant moments at home for a little while. I certainly did not look forward to the time I would have to return home, so I made sure to lengthen my stay.

Amid painful experiences with my mommy, she could also be a gentle and loving person. She rescued a few female members of our family from rural areas. She would bring them into our home and teach them how to become young ladies.

If anyone were hungry, my mommy would feed them. If anyone needed clothes, she would provide them. She opened our home to care for disabled babies and children until they were well. What an amazing woman she was, even in her times of despair.

Mommy was able to reach out and love on others. This is what she taught me. Because she expresses extended love, those teachable moments made me who I am today. As a child, I watched and learned and found the presence of a wounded angel.

My maternal grandmother, Francis, was living during this time, and she was a hairdresser. She and my little aunt did not live far away, so I would pay a visit on Saturdays to get my hair washed, pressed, and curled. Pressing was straightening kinky hair by heating a metal comb and combing through the hair until it was straight. I remember her burning my ear and even dropping the comb down my back.

I noticed she would cry a lot, and I did not understand why. I did not know at the time how she was cast down because of her lifestyle. She was a singer and traveled. She was also in a great deal of pain.

My grandmother and her daughter, Denise, eventually came to live with us. This was a painful transition because I had to share my bedroom with them. Some nights I would hear my grandmother crying herself to sleep.

Abuse for me came in many forms. Amidst the physical and mental abuse, I also experienced sexual abuse. My dad's best friend was one of the individuals who attacked me when I was a little girl. This man would visit our home and sit next to me while I practiced the piano, pretending to befriend me.

We would visit his home, and I would play with his daughter, who was close to my age. He took this opportunity to ask me to play his piano. He would sit beside me and begin to grope me repeatedly. This was so uncomfortable, and I did not know how to manage it. I desperately wondered what I could do to make him stop. When I could not stand it any longer, I told my mommy.

I was so relieved that she listened and moved on to it. She confronted my dad, informing him this man was no longer welcome in our home and I would not visit his home again. What was hurtful was how my dad changed toward me. Because I was a daddy's girl, this was devastating. The abuser was not called on the carpet because he was a prominent leader in the city. He continued to attack others and was not reported, but he was finally caught.

When I think of how my mommy listened and did not make me feel guilty, this gave me a sense of peace. I rarely saw this side of her, but it was ever so welcoming.

"The Lord is my rock and my fortress rock, in whom I take refuge, my shield, and the horn of my salvation, my stronghold" - *Psalm 18:2 (ESV)*

CHAPTER 3

The Teenager, Adventures and Safe Haven

When I was thirteen, I transitioned from piano lessons to organ lessons. God was adding to my life yet another talent to be used for His Glory. So much healing took place every time I had the opportunity of sitting and either practice or ministering.

Every summer, our Sunday school would take a trip to Buckroe Beach, Virginia. This was one of the highlights of my summer. The night before, mommy would fry chicken and make deviled eggs. Denise and I would try on our bathing suits and pack our bags for the big trip. Early on Saturday morning, we would rise, and off to the church we would go to board the buses.

I remember one of the trips to the beach began with a train ride from Main Street Station. We would not sleep all night because we were anticipating riding the trains. Oh, what a marvelous time we had.

We were always excited to take a trip! Although we would hear very loud sounds from a bus load of intoxicated adults arriving as we were leaving, they were having the time of their lives, and we would see them every year.

One day I came home from school, and there were people in my home, wondering why. This scene took me back to my great-grandmother's death. Yes, there had been another death. While my grandmother was taking care of a client in the client's home, my grandmother laid down to take a nap, and the client's family member came home and found her dead. Later, the autopsy revealed she had a heart attack in her sleep.

God saw fit to provide me with yet another great person in my life. My great uncle Henry was one of my rescuers. He was such a sweet, sweet spirit. He drove a tractor-trailer, and he would stop by when he returned from some of his trips. As I would walk home from school, I would see his sixteen-wheeler, and joy leaped in my heart.

I spent quite a few weekends at his home, and I remember him making delicious rolls for Sunday morning breakfast and fried fish. I would eat until I was miserable, then go off to church. He had a daughter, Jackie, who was my age. She was that cousin who I looked up to because she was so pretty and confident. She was my shero, so I wanted to be just like her. She had two younger sons, Bubba and Boo-Boo. I always thought Uncle Henry's wife, Aunt Eunice, was mean, but you could see her smiling on the other side of her fussing. She loved roses, and to this day, I love them just as she did. They remind me of her whenever I am in the garden, pruning them or looking at their beauty.

"Children are a blessing and a gift from the Lord." - Psalm 127:3 (CEV)

I could sometimes be rebellious, and this was one of those times. I was a tall and skinny teenager developing physically at a normal speed despite having to wear uncomfortable corrective shoes for my fallen arches. What I had to wear was not working for me anymore. At that time, being in middle school, I wanted to look like the other girls, so I would hide my cute shoes in my briefcase and change them when I arrived at the bus stop.

One day, I left those awkward shoes on the city bus. My mommy called the bus depot, and lo and beheld, they had the shoes, so we made a trip, and on my feet, they went. My cute shoes were worn only to church on Sundays.

Here are another one of those times. I remember receiving a drenching from the garden hose because I backtalked my mommy when I was supposed to be hanging clothes on the line. This was the day I traveled by city bus to my organ teacher's home, but a young man was waiting to ride the bus with me.

WHEW! This was so painful, but what hurt the most was that my hair got wet and made an afro before they were popular, and the fact that a young man was waiting for me was humiliating—knowing he would see me in this way. I persevered without comment from him.

Later that year, at the tender age of sixteen, I became a pianist for my church and the neighborhood church and shared my gift with these congregations. As I reflect, I was able to see that music was beginning to be my source of peace. I would lose myself, not even recognizing what was happening, but GOD!

I was a daddy's girl and would tag along with him to church events, and during one of those events, I became the youngest member of the senior choir that he directed at our church. I sang in the alto section of the choir. From then on, I sang alto and to this day am so grateful.

My dad not only directed the choir but was also the taxicab driver for the little old ladies (Ms. Glover and Mrs. Bibbs) who sang in the choir. He would pick them up with me in tow, and after choir rehearsal, he would take them home.

Our family never sat for a meal without my dad sitting at the head of the table. I was taught how to set the table and then wait. On those warm days, I would ride my bike to the bus stop and wait for him. I was a happy camper when I saw him emerge from the bus. I really loved him and knew just how special he was to me.

I remember after dinner, he would get into his favorite recliner, and once he was asleep, I would climb into his lap and nap as well. This was a haven and a wonderful, loving place to be. I also sat on the couch with my mommy and placed my head on her lap. I remember her apron with its colorful flowers. What a wonderful place to be because I could experience her loving demeanor, which was so warm and inviting, even though it was short-lived.

I attended many conventions with my dad, participated in the choirs, and began using my talent. I became quite interested in public speaking, which began with reading and reciting during special programs. I not only did this in my church but also with the Baptist General Convention's Youth Division. This was preparation for my life's work.

I remember desiring to have my dad tell me he was proud of me. I watched and listened as he encouraged a young man who was the pianist as we were preparing for one of the conventions. I was also determined to get this type of attention, so I learned to play and memorized James Weldon Johnson's "Lift Every Voice and Sing" and finally gained that attention. To this day, this is the only song that I have memorized. I told myself that if God did it, he could surely do it again.

Growing up, I loved reading books, especially bible stories, and I became immersed in a bible story about a lady named Dorcas, who was known for her good works and acts of charity. She was a generous person who sewed for others and gave to the needy. She was also called a disciple of Jesus, a follower who learned from Him and part of the inner circle in the early church. I studied my Sunday school lessons and had parts to recite when it was time for Christmas and Easter plays.

My mommy was my coach through learning the music, songs, and recitations for my healing and all for the Glory of God. Here again, God was at work in me, but I had no idea what was happening but did as I was told.

Obedience is a way of God's preparation and His love being manifested even amid any pain we may be experiencing. He is always at work. His plan for our lives is always at the forefront of His mind.

During my adolescent years, I felt like an outcast, primarily because of my insecurities about not having a biological mother or father. My last name was different from that of my parents, plus they were much older than my classmates' parents.

I matriculated through high school, not feeling as if I fit, but I did the absolute best I could. My grades were not particularly good, so I went to summer school every year. I found out at the last minute that I did not have enough credits to graduate with my class. Oh, how disappointing that was.

My dear girlfriend, by the name of Rachel Davenport, whose home was also a haven. Her family extended affection and love to me. I was made to feel like family. This was where I retreated while she attended our graduation ceremony. I helped her mother prepare for the graduation party, and she made me feel as if I marched too. After attending summer school, I received my diploma in the mail.

My love for music was so great that I desired to continue my studies by attending the Peabody Conservatory of Music and become a concert pianist. This was not my mom's desire for me because she stated that I would not make a decent living.

I asked her about becoming a flight attendant, coupled with business courses. There was a school that had everything to help me achieve this goal. We traveled to Maryland for the interview, and I was accepted, only to find out later the school had gone bankrupt.

Smithdeal Massey Business College in Richmond allowed me to attend tuition-free because they knew the situation. This was not my ideal educational choice, but it worked.

"Do not fear, for I am with you. Do not be afraid, for I am your God. I will give you strength, and for sure, I will help you. Yes, I will hold you up with My right hand that is right and good." – Isaiah 41:10 (NLV)

"Train up a child in the way he should go, and when he is old, he will not turn from it." - Proverbs 22:6 - (NKJV)

Chapter 4

A Priceless Gift

The writing of this chapter began on the anniversary of my son's death. That was God's leading, causing me to know that it was time to put pencil to paper. God was releasing me to share the story of this chapter of my life.

It all began when I found out that I was pregnant at the age of eighteen. I had just started attending business school and realized something was happening in my body.

The day began as usual, with my boyfriend picking me up and taking me to school, but he was extremely stressed that morning as he informed me that his parents knew I was pregnant because he had told them. Well, it was my turn to tell my parents. I was so scared of what I would receive once this news was shared.

My boyfriend and I sat in his car outside of the school with me, crying uncontrollably, but we made that trip back to my home. My mom was in the kitchen cooking, and I asked her if she would come into the living room. When she did, she took a seat and began looking at the fear on our faces.

When I shared that I was pregnant, she got up, went back into the kitchen, and went back to school.

When I returned home, I went directly to my room and slept. My mom eventually came upstairs, and her comments were, "You laid down with him, didn't you, so why are you crying?" Well, she was talking to me and did not throw anything at my head.

As time passed, there was a meeting held in my home with his parents and mine. While they met in the living room, I sat in the dining room, listening to them plan our wedding ceremony. Strange how nobody asked us what we wanted. I suppose it was because they were thinking about themselves and the embarrassment it would bring them. I was having a baby out of wedlock which was a no-no.

There was a ceremony planned to take place on May 1, 1971, in the church library. I can vividly remember my dad instructing my mom to pick him up from work, and he would dress at the church. He did not want his employer to know what was going on.

I remember wearing my Easter dress as my wedding attire and can remember the looks on the faces of all who attended. They looked so sad, and I looked scared. The service proceeded, and we all returned to my home. We celebrated as best as they referred to us as Mr. and Mrs. Wow! That was funny to hear.

I returned to school and my husband to his job. Even though there was so much tension in my home, we all managed the best we could, and I remember sitting on the couch by my mom and placing my head in her lap as I did at times in the past. I often wondered what she was thinking at that time since I was expecting.

This brought back memories of her pregnancy and my mother's. It may have made her reflect on my mom's death as well. She may have felt responsible for me and needed to ensure I was taken care of. These are thoughts I was having because nothing was said.

There were so many secrets, and most were taken to the grave. These secrets were the key to questions I had and deserved answers to. I realized that if God wants me to know, He will enlighten me.

It was Sunday morning and time to prepare for church. My mom informed me that my dad said my husband and I should attend another Sunday church. My mom started for us to attend our church. We did, and it was announced that we were a married couple and to stand. WOW! How embarrassing. Looking back, I can only imagine what the church people were thinking.

The next week moved right along, but I noticed my mom was suffering from heartburn quite often. On that Thursday evening, I attended choir rehearsal as usual, and when I arrived home, she asked me where the hair grease was. I replied that it was in its usual place, but she disagreed. I was a little frustrated and went to bed.

Early the next morning, my dad was standing at the base of the stairs yelling my name, saying, "Van, something is the matter with Louise." Frightened, I went running down the steps with my husband following me. My husband went to her side of the bed to check on her and performed CPR. I retreated to our bedroom, scared out of my mind.

The paramedics were called, as was the funeral home. She had died. Oh, my goodness – what am I going to do now? This was horrible. It was the week after I got married, and the only mother I had ever known died. The service was planned, and now it is the day of her funeral. I wanted to view her body but was not allowed to because of my pregnancy. This was a practice that was in place at that time.

Time was moving slowly, and I was feeling so lost and alone. We buried mommy on Mother's Day (May 9, 1971), right after our regular church service. I was now the woman of the house, trying to fill her shoes as a homemaker, but was failing miserably because I was not a good cook. But I could clean. My dad went back to work but was extremely sad. I was pregnant five months pregnant and trying to move along without her guidance, but it was tough.

There was always a man who would come to our home. His name was Mr. Roundtree. He was our insurance agent, and he would collect our policy premiums. Mom had already informed him that I was now married and needed to add my husband to our policy. Once the baby was born, he too was to be added to the policy, thinking this would be a good help financially once he was college-bound.

After the death of my mommy, I experienced more emotional abuse, as my daddy accused me of being the cause of her death. He stated it was due to my pregnancy. At nineteen, I did not know how I processed such a heavy load. I did not see this as his grief talking but as an attack on me. I had no idea what to do. I felt lost and afraid.

Life was moving right along, and my tummy was growing each day. My cousins took me to my prenatal appointments, and the baby was doing well. It was amazing to hear the heartbeat and the baby moving. I often watched the baby move from one side of my stomach to the other. This, to me, was ever so amazing.

I completed my studies, but once again, I was informed that I would not march because I was short one credit. To my amazement, my cousin Jackie informed me that my name was called along with the other graduates, but of course, I was absent. The school mailed my diploma.

Chapter 5

The Mother

Well, it was an early Thursday morning, September 30, 1971. I was having strange feelings and discovered I was in labor. While waiting to go to the hospital, my cousins stopped by on their way to school. I shared with them what was happening, and it was hilarious how quickly they left the house.

I remember arriving at the hospital and being prepared for delivery. I was placed in a waiting room by myself and sat in a wheelchair. The pains were coming rapidly. All I had was a cabinet in front of me, and I would kick it repeatedly until the pain ceased.

I shared the labor room with another mother who scared me to death because she was moaning and groaning. All I could think about was if this were going to be me. I watched her in terror while the nurse placed a washcloth on her forehead. I felt so all alone, which was very familiar to me. This was how I felt when mommy died. I remember wondering what I would do now that I was pregnant. Who would I rely on? Who would comfort me when I am afraid? Yes, I was married, but I needed a motherly presence. Fathers were not allowed in the labor room.

I finally received the wonder drug, the infamous epidural, and before you knew it, I had given birth to a healthy baby boy, who weighed 6 lbs. and 7 oz. I am in awe of this miracle but more concerned about not being able to feel anything from my waist down.

It dawned on me that the epidural had numbed me. I finally understood the lady in my room earlier who had no control over her leg falling off the bed.

I became a mother. Wow, what an accomplishment! I had a little person to care for, and his name was Larry Bernard Jones, Jr. He had a head full of hair, the cutest dimples, and little dark lips. My cousin, Lynwood, who has those dark lips, teased me so much during my pregnancy that he passed them on to my baby.

The family came to visit, and it was time for me to leave the hospital. We went off to my mother-in-law's home and on to a new normal. She would not allow me to do anything for the baby, and because she had a cold, she wore a mask so she would not breathe on him.

When returning home, my dad was so very caring, as if this baby had given him a lift in his spirit. I remember laying the baby on my mom's side of the bed and watching him sleep as my dad slept. This has been embedded in my memory for all these years.

Life was moving along, and we fell in love with this little one. The church members loved him as well, but one lady vexed his spirit for some reason because whenever she took him, he would yell like someone was hurting him.

We attended a birthday party on a Saturday evening when our son was three months old. I remember an older gentleman who was the honoree holding the baby and stating how special he was.

We returned home, and I prepared him for bed. He did not wake up during the night, which I thought was strange, so I took that to mean he was too tired. Early the next morning, I got up to prepare for church but stopped at the crib first. His little arm was hanging out of the bed, and when I moved him, he did not respond. I felt like the room was spinning. I touched him again, and he still did not move. I remember screaming to the top of my lungs, which woke my husband up. He proceeded to the baby's crib, and he took him out.

He laid him on our bed and began chest compressions and breaths. I walked around the room in circles, not knowing what to do. The fear I felt was overwhelming. I waited for our baby to gasp for air, but he did not. Have mercy, Lord.

My Aunt Denise came into our room and took him downstairs, placing him on my dad's bed. This was not looking good. My husband came into the room and began chest compressions and breaths again. We wrapped him in a blanket, and off to the hospital, we went. My husband drove, and I held the baby. My cousins (Lynwood and Bessie) met us at the emergency door, and we all went in. The nurse took the baby in the back to be examined. I sat in the waiting room in total shock. It felt like life had stood still. We waited and waited, and when the physician came out, he informed us our baby had died. He also stated there would be an autopsy performed. Oh, how devastating.

There was an ounce of hope that they could bring him back. I was in complete disbelief… Our baby was dead… Oh My God, what were we going to do? I remember feeling numb, bewildered, alone, and frightened. Our baby died on January 9, 1972.

An innocence I cannot explain. I was in my own lonely, fearful, and isolated world. He was my perfect gift from God. Why God called him home, I do not know. What I do know is that I needed him. God favored me if only for three months.

"But we do not want you to be uninformed, brothers, about those who are asleep, that you may not grieve as others do who have no hope." - 1 Thessalonians 4:13(ESV)

Here we found ourselves preparing for another funeral. Our baby boy was going to be buried. We took his outfit to the funeral home, and my heart sunk when they called for us to come and view his body. When we arrived at the funeral home, a lady was standing by his casket with tears in her eyes.

I looked at him with his blue terrycloth-like white outfit on. A string around the outfit's waist ran through his hand as if he were holding it. He just looked as if he were asleep. The disbelief was so heavy that I could not do anything but stare at him. I broke down and cried. Why? Why? Why?

We were preparing for the graveside service on Monday, January 10, 1972. On January 11, they placed his white coffin in the back of the lead car, and we followed in the family car.

When we arrived at the cemetery gate, the driver had a challenging time maneuvering the car, and someone in our car said that Mommy was messing with the driver. Well, we arrived at his plot, and I could see my birth mother's grave, my mommy's grave, my nanny's grave, and the graves of other family members.

Once it was all said and done, we retreated to our home, and as I sat in the dining room, I began to polish the silverware on the buffet. It kept me busy and not have to converse with anyone. I did not have the energy to entertain. My mother-in-law stated that my mommy took the baby because she knew I would not know how to take loving care of him. When she said that, I wanted to scream, but I had to consider the source. She was known to speak her mind without thinking about how it may affect someone. How inappropriate and how hurtful. I continued to stay focused on my mission.

The Mother

My Tribute

When I first saw your little face,
I swelled with pride at your beauty and grace,
Many years have gone by; O this day I still ask myself why.
I often wonder what you would look like.
How your voice would sound.
Would you take more after me or your father?
When I think of you, I often feel sad.
I cry and dream of the times we could have had.
Just to think you would be all grown up now,
and I would be just amazed at you.
You were the gift of life that was like no other.
If you look into these eyes, you will see the love of a mother.
Not a day goes by that I don't feel your heart;
for your heart and mine are one.
There have been times when I wondered if my faith was strong enough,
And when it really mattered my faith carried me through,
Even in the toughest time of my life—losing.
Although our time was much too short,
your memory fests right here in my heart.
One of the most beautiful sights in the world is that of a sleeping child,
and that is where Mommy left you.
Sleep well son, I will forever think of you.
Mommy loves you more with each tear that falls.

Angela M. Weaver, 8/24/08

Chapter 6

The Motherless

Days and weeks passed, and the sadness in the house was so great. As difficult as it was, I began to gather the dirty clothes to take them to the laundromat. While sorting the clothes, a lady at the laundromat noticed the baby clothes and asked how old the baby was. I had to tell her he died at the age of three months. Can you imagine how I felt saying that?

We tried to move along with life, but the pain was devastating. My then-husband began to drink excessively to numb the pain, but it added to the grief that altered his disposition, and he became violently abusive. I did not know what to do or to whom to turn. He was fighting on his job, especially if anyone approached him the wrong way.

This was a quiet man, but our son's death consumed him, and he had no idea how to manage his loss. I did not know what to say or how to act. I was stuck in this awful place in my life. I could not pray because I was so angry with God for taking my mommy and now my son. Certainly, He did not love me, I thought.

Because our son died suddenly, there was an investigation to ensure this was not murdered to collect the life insurance money. They found no evidence of foul play. Once we received the money, we moved into our apartment and ran through the life insurance like it was water. We furnished our entire apartment and purchased a lot of unnecessary items.

My husband was soon drafted into the Army. All I thought about was the fact that he was leaving me. I wondered where God's love for me was. How much more could I take? I was heartbroken, lost, and confused. I had no idea where to turn or to whom to turn. I felt so defeated and so unloved.

Two wounded young people in a state of despair are trying to figure out how to move forward with the pain in their hearts. The relationship became increasingly abusive, and the marriage eventually dissolved.

Here I was, living in our apartment and a deep state of depression, to the point that I could not get out of bed and go to work daily. I was fired from jobs during this period of my life. I had no money or food in the apartment. My refrigerator contained a bottle of water and a box of feminine hygiene products. When I mustered enough energy, I made it to the local store and stole food. The feelings of isolation and loneliness were ever so present. I felt as if I was nothing.

I was eventually evicted from the apartment and sat on a hill, watching my furniture being set out on the curb—what a horrible scene to view. I had no idea where I could go and what to do with all my furniture.

While sitting in the car, a man approached the driver's side and pointed a gun at my head through the window. I had been informed that he had stolen some of my items. He stated if I told the police, he would kill me. WHEW!

A friend let me use her car to transport the small items to a former neighbor's vacant home. A neighbor took me in. In exchange for room and board, I would watch her children. This arrangement was short-lived. One evening while I was sleeping on the couch, she decided to join me. This was not going to work. I brushed her off, gathered my belongings the next morning, and left.

I took my bags and went to my dad's, only to find out that he did not want me to stay there. So, he suggested I stay with my Aunt Ella, who lived in Jackson Ward. That is where I ended up. I was not working and had no income, so I laid around with the neighbors and used the food stamps they gave me. This was quite different from what I thought life would be.

One evening I needed a ride to a Christmas Choir holiday party, and this man's wife sent him to pick me up. On our way to the event, he decided to show me sexually explicit magazines, which made me extremely uncomfortable. Again, it was from a man who was close to my dad.

While traveling to the event, he took an off-the-beat route to a park setting. My heart started pounding. I was so afraid and uncomfortable. He reached over and began to grope me, but I fought, and I fought hard. Even though it was dark outside, I tried to open the door to escape but could not. I was thinking to myself, how can I get out of this situation. I was scared, nervous, and bewildered.

Once he realized he fought on his hand, he stopped and drove to the event. He told me not to tell his wife, and life for me would be hard if I did. Well, of course, I said nothing and continued to attend church as usual. I was so miserable I had to tell my dad eventually.

My dad was the Sunday School Superintendent, and I met him in his office at the church. I informed him I was leaving the church and why. I shared with him my experience in detail. I wanted him to know and try to understand how painful this experience was. He looked at me and uttered these words, "men will be men."

I was floored and walked out of his office and out of the church, not to return until my dad's death years later. How many girls keep this information to themselves out of fear of ridiculing? How many suffer in silence, affecting their innermost being? This was the second time my dad rejected my experience and turned a deaf ear. I felt too rejected and unloved.

After interviews and so many rejections, I finally began to work, which helped my aunt, but the time came for me to move on. I met a nice gentleman and began to play for his family church. This young man, I thought, was the answer to my prayers.

I was quite comfortable and became pregnant during this time, but the baby's father, due to his insecurities, did not want it. He was determined to believe it was somebody else's child. As I tried to convince him that the baby was his, he did not want to believe it. The pregnancy did not last long because he insisted on me getting an abortion, so I did, which added to my depression. I was heartbroken and again felt alone and afraid.

During this relationship, I had an incredibly respectable job, and one day while at lunch, I decided to walk to Thalhimers Department Store. While walking through the store, there stood a gentleman from my home church. He approached me and ushered me outside to inform me that I was under arrest. Of course, I was shocked. While sitting in the squad car, one of my co-workers recognized me and cried uncontrollably.

This gentleman was a detective who placed me in a squad care's backseat and went off to jail. Oh, how embarrassing. The tormenting process of being fingerprinted and photographed was grueling. I was placed in a cell with a prostitute who kept looking at me. I was scared out of my mind. When the magistrate called my name, I recognized him as well. He was also a member of my home church.

The arrest was due to a forgery that I was not responsible for, and the charges were dropped. The entire process was humiliating, and of course, I lost my job. The co-worker who saw me in the police ran back to work to inform my boss. Who would hire me now that I have an arrest record? The grace of God was on my life, and gaining employment was never an issue.

This "nice guy" I was dating became violent, and the relationship had taken a toll on me. I felt as if I was a walking zombie. I moved in with my newfound friend I met while I was a musician at the church where her father pastored.

To make matters worse, my roommate wanted me to bait a police officer so that she could feed her drug habit. I might have been naïve, but I was not a dummy. When she came to me with her scheme, I reneged.

The Motherless

The apartment was junky, and to top it off, she had a little dog who would urinate on the carpet in the room where I slept and on my bed. The smell was unbearable, but what was I to do? I kept the window open with a Rite-Guard can during the day to keep the stench down.

I just wanted to die because of all the losses in my life. My marriage fell apart, and the pain of losing my son was unbearable. My pain was so great, and I wanted it all to end. I was tired of the abuse, not only from men but women as well. I was also tired of living with an aching heart. I was in a horrible cycle of bad relationships, constantly trying to find love and acceptance. I just wanted to give up and die. So, I planned exactly when, where, and how I would kill myself.

Looking through a window from the third-floor apartment, I saw the perfect place to take my life. It was where the dumpsters were kept. If I were to jump out of the window and right into one of the dumpsters, no one would notice my body; and when the trash collectors picked up the containers, my body would be taken to the landfill. Those were my thoughts that morning because I was in such a dark place. Suicide would end my pain and suffering.

God stepped in. He would not allow me to kill myself. Instead, he sent an angel to save me. The phone rang several times while I pondered whether to answer it. When I finally did, I recognized the voice immediately. It was y cousin, Bessie Bebbs Johnson, who was married to my cousin Lynwood. Her sweet voice gave me comfort. She has always been that mother figure in my life. She would encourage and scold me, but I always knew she loved me.

She said I had been on her mind and she wanted to remind me that even though my son was gone, I still had a lot of love to share. Even though I was a total mess, I listened to her. I did not know how to take her words, but what I did know was that her call saved my life. I know beyond any doubt God touched her heart to call me.

I regret that I never told her what she did for me. She never knew how she rescued me throughout my childhood by allowing me to spend time in her home. I cannot begin to tell you how many children God has blessed me to share my love with since that day. Amid my pain, I began to work with children. Ministering to them became my life.

Early morning, I felt someone crawl into bed with their hand on my body and me. I also felt an erection, so I knew it was a man. I slowly moved to the edge of the bed, reached for the Rite-Guard can, and gave his penis a whack. A little later, I discovered it was my roommate's boyfriend. He, of course, made up his own story to save himself. While at work, my roommate's neighbor called to inform me my roommate was furious and was coming for me. The neighbor stated that I needed to vacate.

I made sure the coast was clear, returned to pack my bags, and left in a hurry. I moved in with an older lady who was a nurse. She was so good to me. She would have a drink ready when I returned from work and draw my bathwater. One evening she shared her story about a servicemember she was once involved with, but the relationship did not work, so she became bitter about all the men.

She stated, "we girls needed to stick together and forget about men." Well, that was my queue to leave. While waiting for the bus the next day, I ran into an old acquaintance and shared my predicament. She suggested I come and live with her and her husband. After work, I gathered my things and moved across the street, but one morning while sleeping, I heard a pop. My girlfriend shot at her husband, who had been out until the wee hours of the morning. Well, it was time for me to leave again.

My family had no idea just how much pain I was in. I was exceptionally good at hiding it. I was the mask-wearing queen.

"No weapon formed against you shall prosper, and every tongue which rises against you in judgment You shall condemn. This is the heritage of the servants of the Lord, and their righteousness is from Me," says the Lord. - Isaiah 54:17 (NKJV)

I moved in with a co-worker who was a childhood friend. One day I ran across an article about becoming a volunteer, so I decided to volunteer at what was then the Richmond Memorial Hospital. I loved visiting the patients, especially during the holidays. Some could not go home or did not have a family to visit them. Visiting patients allowed me to switch my focus from myself to them, providing an opportunity for me to pour into someone else's life.

During that time in my life, I reunited with a childhood sweetheart, and we married. This relationship contained so much pain not only for me but also for him. There were so many pockets of horrible events wrapped in this volatile family. I became a bonus mother to his son.

There were many trips to whatever state his son was residing in, and because I was so wounded due to my son's death, I poured that love into his son. I was such a needy individual. There was not anything I would not do for his son and family.

Drugs came into our lives, and the downward spiral began. The house parties and the use of marijuana were a mainstay but not to my liking. Here again, I did not fit even though I tried.

I continued working a steady job even though I was still dealing with unresolved pain. I was not always able to make it to work each day, but I did the best I could.

I became a surrogate to my second husband's siblings, not recognizing how unloved and unwanted I was by his other family members. There was so much drama in the family, but I tried to keep the peace and do what I thought was right when trying to help. It was not easy, but I desired to be liked and accepted.

"We are pressed on every side by troubles, but we are not crushed. We are perplexed but not driven to despair. We are hunted down but never abandoned by God. We get knocked down, but we are not destroyed." - 2 Corinthians 4:8-9 (NLT)

My second husband's younger sister had a baby boy, and it was taxing for her to continue to raise him. We took him in with full custody at the age of two. This was a frightening situation because, periodically, his mother would report us to the local police stating that we were abusing him.

The officers came so often that they investigated further into the situation by contacting the mother. They found out that she had a mental illness. Her abuse did not stop there. When her son was a little older, the court stated that she could have supervised visits in her mother's home.

I took him over there for a visit, and when I returned, she and the son's dad left with him. We had no idea where they were. The police were involved, and it was labeled as a kidnapping. This was aired on the television stations with pictures of them both. I was a basket case, not knowing what she and the father were doing to the child. When she saw her picture on the television, she decided to bring him back. I remember driving to her mother's home, and squad cars were all around, waiting for the encounter.

The bus stopped, and she and her son got off. They walked to the house where we were frantically waiting. The police were at the back door waiting to take her in. We stated that all we wanted for her was the desperately needed help. We never found out what happened during that time he was with them. He suffered from mental health issues as well.

During those turbulent years, I was introduced to cocaine and found it my drug of choice. I would not only snort it but also would wash it down with Heineken Beer. This was a daily ritual that allowed me to move throughout my day. The high made me feel normal and enabled me to function.

It got so bad that I began to break out in hives one day. They were all over my body. Wearing clothes was irritating, but I did not stop my drug usage. I suffered from nose bleeds, but this did not make me stop either. I was continually active in the church, singing in the choir but hitting bad notes because the cocaine affected my vocal cords. That, however, was not enough to make me stop.

I finally reached my breaking point and made a call to a hotline. I can remember the young lady asking me if I liked movies. When I told her I did, she suggested I treat myself to a movie. This did not go over well with my husband, but I had to leave the house and take care of myself.

The next day, I had an appointment with a psychiatrist, which was taboo to my husband, but I went anyway. The psychiatrist informed me that I was suffering from clinical depression and on the verge of a nervous breakdown.

When I shared with the psychiatrist the state my husband was in, he informed me that he was a walking time bomb. I had no idea what I needed to do because I could not leave this little boy who had gone through so much. The psychiatrist prescribed Xanax, which was a miracle drug for me. It calmed my anxiety, but the kicker was that my husband took them too. My prescriptions were being filled more often than they should have, but it kept him out of my hair.

I had gone from an illegal drug to a prescribed drug—what a roller-coaster. I eventually suffered a nervous breakdown. I had to stop working and discovered a love for gardening. I felt one with God and His transforming power. God had His hand on me all the while and was pulling me out of the depths of my despair. This was not who I was supposed to be or where I would remain.

Life with my second husband was miserable and toxic, so we went our separate ways but remained amicable to be a stable foundation for our nephew, whose mother eventually committed suicide. The nephew began serving time in prison for the murder of his uncle (my second husband). I stayed in communication with him when it was comfortable for me until he died.

Years passed before I, I mean, began to understand God's love for me. That seed of a resurrected life began to mature. I began to come into the knowledge of God's presence in my life and that I am HIS. Little did I know, God was working it all out. It was He who lifted me from despair. He showed me that my life at the time was not who I was inside.

I gave up the cocaine and continued with my gardening. I am so very thankful to God for rescuing me from myself.

Chapter 7

A New Life

I met my current husband in 1974 on what was a disastrous date. My date called me to get directions to my home. He and another young man picked me up that evening to attend a house party. My date ran a scam on me. It turned out to be date rape. The next day I received a call from my future husband. He introduced himself to me and informed me that he was checking to ensure I was okay; he memorized my telephone number. That was so thoughtful of him, and after a few conversations, I decided to go out with him.

He was attending college at that time and only came home on the weekends, so because of lifestyle differences; we drifted apart. We always managed to run into each other over the years. I remember when his son was born and vividly recall speaking to this cute little voice over the phone.

Years and painful relationships had passed, but in 1997 we were destined to be together for eternity. I knew I would not be able to receive him in the light that God desired because of experiencing so many abusive relationships. The abuse was all I had known when I was a small child. The presence of a man in my life who was not abusive felt so foreign.

I have learned through the years that we attract other wounded souls when we are wounded. I am so grateful to God that I have moved into a better me through the darkness of depression. I recognized that God wanted the absolute best for me and that I would need to want that for myself.

This man provides for me each day of my life. His stability has helped me tremendously. I no longer struggle with feelings of not being worthy of his love. I welcomed every email of scriptures he would send daily to my job. There is nothing that I need. I am living a life of contentment. I am very thankful to God for allowing me to receive such love from this man, my covering.

I also had the opportunity of helping him with raising his son. WOW! God is always up to something. Like I said, "Once a mother, always a mother." It was challenging at first, but we made great strides. I had to ask God how He would have me be in this child's life. God's answer was "be a mother figure." That was exactly what I began to be, and a good life began.

Though an only child, God has blessed me with siblings, thanks to my husband, who is from a large family. I was blessed to have a wonderful relationship with my mother-in-love, who also helped me understand my husband better. She would also inform me that he is a good man. Yes, Mother, he certainly is. When his sisters met me, they stated that I looked familiar. Well, that familiarity was from the 1970s during our brief dating period, and now look how far we have come.

God was in the mix, working things out as only He could. All I had to do was stay connected and be obedient. Oh, it was not easy because there were times I was kicking and screaming to have it my way. God won all those battles.

To be married to a man who does not have a violent temper was not what I was used to. He was aware of my hurtful past and many times allowed me the opportunity to share. He was also aware that he had something on his hands because I would act out if there were something that I disagreed with. He patiently gave me my space, and I am ever so grateful to this day.

A New Life

Seeing him read and study the word and living it is a testament to what God has carved out just for me.

We dated for a brief time, and one morning I asked him what he would do. Of course, he laughed, but I did not see anything funny. So, we decided that we would marry. I contacted Rev. Lawrence B. Samuels, who I adored, and asked him if he would perform the ceremony. Of course, he said yes. We applied for our marriage license and set a date. When we called Rev. Samuels to give a date, he stated that we needed to wed at his home since his wife had just suffered a stroke. I asked my fiancé when he was going to tell his mom. He told me to tell her, and so I did.

We arrived at the pastor's home with our best man, Michael's son Mikey. Mrs. Samuels watched soap operas in another room while we were engaged in a 30-minute marriage counseling session. After the session, I went into the den to ask Mrs. Samuels if she would like to join us, and she nodded yes.

I brought her into the living room as we stood in their foyer and became husband and wife, while one of her soap operas played in the background. This was Friday, June 27, 1997.

Chapter 8

The Visionary

Holidays were still very gloomy for me; I found myself sleeping for hours just to get to the next day, but this time it was different because I woke up from a dream. On January 1, 2002, I received a vision from God to begin a Transition Ministry for Women and Children who were either in an abusive situation or homeless. This ministry would focus on helping to rebuild their lives by offering a haven for them where they would receive healing. The individuals would be nurtured and taught skills to enable them to live productive lives. When I woke up from the dream, I called a girlfriend, Medina Crouch, to share what had transpired.

Medina insisted that I write about the dream. Since writing was not my strong suit, so it wasn't until January 5th, 2002, that I began to journal. I would make daily entries through this process, and it was not complete until November 16, 2003. God helped me make it plain!

"And the Lord answered me, and said, Write the vision, and make it plain upon tables, that "he may run that readeth it." – Habakkuk 2:2 (KJV)

The vision translated into this: several transitional homes throughout the city of Richmond. The first home in the Northside of Richmond, Virginia, where I was raised. Later, three other homes will be built: each in the East End, West End, and the Southside of Richmond. It is my desire for the homes either to be built from the ground up or renovated. The funds supplied to accomplish this will come from researching HUD properties.

Within these homes, individuals could sense the difference in the atmosphere. The homes would be a place of peace where the presence of God would be there to help make a difference. The homes would serve as a haven to help those who are feeling broken and hopeless. They would provide a space where God's beauty surrounds individuals in need. Often, those that are broken need their spirits renewed; the surroundings within the homes will make all the difference in the world. The houses will be their homes for a while, so the mission would be to provide them with strength that when they leave, they will have lifted heads. It will also be a place for those to find comfort and familiarity if they must come back without any issues or judgment.

Within the homes, inspirational poetry and quotes will provide moments of light and hope. These poems and quotes would be provided by a friend of mine, Tewana McMillian. Residents in the homes would see these messages as reminders from God, letting them know how special and loved they are. Along with words of inspiration, there will be natural items from the garden to add touches to the home.

The name of the first house will be "The Bowers House." The goal of the Bowers House program is to equip the residents with the knowledge, skills, and emotional support needed to move them to an appropriate level of self-sufficiency. The program will offer independent living education, family skills development, career and educational guidance, childcare, individual and family counseling, and permanent housing assistance. The focus will be to reach those who have lost their way, regardless of age or parental status.

The residents will be responsible for the upkeep of the property. It will be their temporary home, and they will be taught to take pride in what belongs to them. Once they are on their feet, they will be well prepared to care for what belongs to them.

In the homes, daycare will be provided for the children. The daycare will be professionally staffed. The children will be given the best care. There will be an infirmary in each home. They will always be staffed with a nurse. A physician on staff will work in all the locations and assist with the residents' complete physical health.

I will pray for God's divine direction and seek His guidance and discernment about who will live in the homes. Once the women have completed the entrance assessment and become residents, the length of their stay will be managed individually. We will need to be sensitive to each personal situation. The length of stay will also depend on how well they progress through the programs and where they are in the healing process.

The residents will be given the Rules and Regulations of the home. More rules and regulations may be added. If residents do not adhere, they will be counseled individually and reprimanded accordingly.

The mandatory Bible Study during the week is so essential. It will allow them to reignite their faith in God and teach them the importance of daily prayer and meditation. Bibles will be donated by Christian-based bookstores. Each Sunday, all the homes will worship together at one central church. There will be a listing of churches provided that will embrace this ministry.

The residents will also attend skill learning and enhancement classes that will help fine-tune their skills to prepare for their working future. More may be added. The length of the courses has not been determined. Where the courses will be taught has also not been determined.

By reaching out to the community, I will work with Christian-based businesses, both retail and restaurants, which will play important roles in the lives of the residents. These businesses will provide food for the homes, opportunities for employment, and training for the residents.

The instructors must be filled with spirit and have a passion for people. The pool will be made of retired educators willing to volunteer their time and talents. Students pursuing an educational degree and would like to student-teach or any persons with the fervent desire to help are also welcome. If training is needed for those with that desire, they will receive what they need to facilitate.

The instructors must also team up with other instructors and pray daily. A weekly or bi-weekly briefing will be conducted to stay abreast of the progress or concerns that may arise. If there are situations that need immediate attention, those will be managed more expeditiously.

Commencement will be held each year for the residents as they complete the required courses. The commencement will be spectacular, with bells and whistles. That day would mark the beginning of a new life that may not have been possible if they had continued to be ignored.

As the residents prepare to move out on their own, the foundation will assist with helping them search for housing, whether it be an apartment or purchasing a home. The foundation will also assist with furnishing one room in their home as a gift.

Once they are on their feet, the foundation will require each person to give back to the foundation in any way they see fit. I can see individuals returning to teach, preach, counsel, build new homes, and even continue once I have retired. When we look back, we should give back.

The Christian counselor assigned to the residents will contact them after a certain passage of time to check on their progress and to lend any assistance. The length of time has not been established. If one is experiencing any kind of setback, they are to contact the foundation immediately.

I wrote the vision, and only God knows when all of this will unfold. I have been obedient and captured what He has placed on my heart. Each day that I live, God continues to reveal to me why I am the way I am and have been since I can remember and why I have such a heart for those who otherwise would be cast aside.

We will continue to stay on task as God would have it. Our prayer is to stay focused and be ready when God blesses us with our very first home. We praise His Holy Name for choosing us.

While thinking about a name for the organization, on February 28, 2002, my friend, Medina, suggested the name The Delores Foundation (TDF). She has also designed the foundation's business cards and website. The foundation has been named after my birth mother. I pay homage to my mother, Delores Bowers, each time I sign my name, Vanessa Bowers Carter.

The TDF logo

God has allowed me to reach out to those who need a loving touch, and I thank Him for this gift. God continues to unite me with those who will eventually become a part of this ministry. He has been connecting me to individuals and businesses since that day of the vision.

In fact, on November 14, 2003, God dropped several ladies in my spirit as a part of this ministry. I contacted each of them, and they agreed to come on board. They were Medina Crouch, Trina Boyd, Kim Gray, Neila Gunter, and Diane Vasquez.

What was so amazing is that they each brought something different to the table and possessed a profound love for God and humankind. It was time for me to re-introduce this ministry to the ladies and leave the rest up to God.

On November 16, 2003, God allowed the foundation to start receiving clothes to assist ladies and children. I had no idea there would be someone just around the corner who needed our assistance, but lo and behold, we were able to bless a young lady and her son; a family of six, consisting of a mother and five children; and an entire family of seven, consisting of the mother, father and five children. Praise God!

On July 23, 2009, The Delores Foundation became a non-profit organization. We are made up of an Executive Board and an Advisory Board. God has expanded us by adding volunteers to assist with His work, and we Praise God for His Love.

Today the foundation is promoting the HOPE Empowerment Program, which represents Helping Others Pursue Excellence. The program facilitates creative avenues for young ladies, ages 10 – 17, to heal, grow and mature into healthy and productive young adults through effective programs, resources, and partnerships.

In addition to providing much-needed food items, personal care, and hygiene products, Project H.O.P.E. provides backpacks (and care packages) to the homeless.

I continue to praise God for the vision.

Chapter 9

The Deliverance

God called five friends to unite in song. They were Sherry Easter, Josandra Faniel, Evette Williams, Monica Murray, and me. We answered the call, not knowing what was ahead of us. He so lovingly opened doors for us to minister through song throughout the city of Richmond as well as out of state. We decided to name ourselves "Just Friends" because that is who we were, but as elevation happened, we became "Ecclesia."

We ministered at a church that we considered our home away from home, and after the service ended, I proceeded to get in my car to leave. The pastor stopped me and motioned me to roll down the window, and I did. He said, "You're it." I looked at him with a frown and asked him to repeat himself, and he did. He then told me to contact him when I delivered my initial sermon.

My legs felt like rubber, and I had to drive home. I can only imagine what I looked like – a big mess, I am sure. My friends in Ecclesia asked me what was wrong, and I told them what he had said. Their comment was, "Why are you so surprised?" Then they all went to their cars, leaving me alone and feeling lost. I could not help wondering why others could see things about me that I could not.

All this time, I could not get enough of the Word. I read the Bible more than usual. Television evangelists became my best friends. I began to cry uncontrollably, and I just could not figure out what the problem could be. I am not an incredibly quiet person, but suddenly, I was silent.

I asked myself, "What on earth is going on?" Strangers, for some unknown reason, began to gravitate to me even more. They began to spot me and share their life story with me. I began to wonder if I looked strange or something.

No, it was God using me. Praise His Holy Name. I began feeling alone again and not fitting in. These were feelings I had not experienced for years. What concerned me the most was "Ecclesia" because these were the sisters that God made for me. Even before we sang together, we were sisters in the Lord and remarkably close. So, why was I feeling so alone?

One of the girls in the group, Cookie, shared with us a visitation she had. In that visitation, God had instructed her to tell me that He loved me. From that day on, I finally began to feel loved.

I began running the last lap to get to where I am today. One evening in October 2003, while sitting in my favorite spot on the side of the bed, crying, as usual, I fell to my knees and surrendered. I could not fight any longer. It was not an issue that I was no longer attending my former church. I knew God would direct and take care of everything.

Once I surrendered, God began to reveal why I had to experience all that I did. My faith in Him has increased ever since. I know that even though man will try, there is nothing man can do to harm me. I know God loves me and that I do not need anyone's acceptance. I came to understand why I felt so out of place – because God was molding and shaping me into who He desired me to be.

God has called me to minister to the hurting, to those who think that they have no hope. The Father has delivered me and given me a voice to share my testimony. I praise His Holy Name. Studying the Word and absorbing it through and through equips me to understand better who God is and who I am.

I worked around extremely negative people, and I felt uncomfortable, but I loved my job. I prayed and asked God to show me how I could be a blessing in their lives. He guided me not to be discouraged and commanded that when I notice people struggling for some reason or another, I should give them the gift of prayer and a listening ear.

Co-workers then began to approach me with their problems and ask for prayers. At first, I did not know what was going on. It wasn't that I was flattered; I just wondered, "Why me?" I was promoted from a customer service position to a trainer's position with the Virginia Retirement System, where I began to travel and deliver presentations. In delivering complex information, I noticed I could make people feel comfortable.

I met a young lady, Trina Daniels, who was hired as a technical writer. Her desk was close to mine. There was a presence about her that was infectious, and I could not understand it at first. We began to talk and quickly realized our shared love of the Lord. As our relationship grew, I shared with her how people are drawn to me to pour out their hearts and ask me to pray for them.

I shared with her that I was considering looking into Christian Counseling. She agreed and began to help me search for schools. One day, she turned to me and said, very matter-of-factly, that I would attend seminary. I was not feeling that at all. I thought seminary was too deep for me. But my friend also shared her belief that there was a calling on my life and that I needed to pray about it. I ignored her for a few days.

I set up a meeting with Dean John Kinney with Virginia Union University, Samuel Dewitt Proctor School of Theology, which was not my idea at all. I just wanted to get his idea of how to move forward with my education based on what I gained from God.

Well, that meeting was interesting as Dean stated that I would need to attend VUU. I remember my legs shaking as I listened to him because I did not see myself as seminary-worthy, but God had a plan, and oh, did His plan work. I shared with him that I did not have my bachelor's degree, and he stated that was not an issue and that I would be a part of Special Admissions. He provided the application and shared with me all the steps.

In all of what we do and what God has for us, there is nothing new on the face of the earth. I had a thirst for knowledge. With an open heart and mind, I was about to embark upon this educational journey. I enrolled in seminary.

"Be diligent to present yourself approved to God, a worker who does not need to be ashamed, rightly dividing the word of truth." - II Timothy 2:15 (NKJV)

I provided all the necessary documents and was accepted. I was to complete the first year of studies to see if I could complete college-level work, and I passed with excellence. I was welcomed as a Master's level student.

Some of my classes went over my head, but some were windows of opportunity to read and to learn more through in-depth studies of the Bible. One of the classes that really got my attention was Pastoral Counseling. I knew I had landed on rich soil in that class. I could connect to all the studies because this was my ministry calling.

In the last year of seminary, a classmate and I decided to earn credit by developing a program under the direction of our Pastoral Counseling professor. Since both of us were enthusiastic about ministering to persons grieving, we developed grief training and titled it "Your Extended Support System." We understood that grieving people often develop physical symptoms such as abdominal pain, headaches, insomnia, fatigue, changes in appetite, increased drug or alcohol use, restlessness, absentmindedness, and poor concentration. Because of grief, people often struggle with the ability to function after loss.

The mission was to be a resource for those experiencing grief due to a critical loss and to provide training to those who will aid grieving individuals through the grief process. Each person's experience of loss and grief responses are unique. However, there are common feelings and symptoms often experienced by the grieving. These include sadness, betrayal, anxiety, fear, mistrust, irritability, guilt, anger, tension, depression, and loss of confidence.

The services of Y.E.S.S. will support these issues: grief counseling, training, and workshops. Y.E.S.S. will also produce materials to aid and support the grief recovery process.

Once completed, we presented it to our professor, who was grieving the loss of his mother. He wiped his eyes toward the end of our presentation and stated that we had not just completed an assignment but had also created a ministry piece.

With that said, my classmate and I have presented Y.E.S.S. to our respective churches. Our churches moved forward with it becoming a part of Congregational Care. Y.E.S.S. would provide caring support and understanding of grief as well as other areas of healing. The ministry would provide spiritual and emotional support to those experiencing grief.

Partnering in Life – Occasionally, organizations must deal with employees who are grief-stricken by the sickness or loss of a loved one or by a great tragedy, such as the September 11 terrorist attacks. Most organizations offer bereavement leave for employees, but the weeks or months after a death or tragedy can be a tough time. The difficulty can last longer than just the immediate moments surrounding the death. Y.E.S.S. will partner with the organization's Human Resources Department in establishing support services to meet the needs of these individuals.

Under Y.E.S.S., there is "A Safe Place" (ASP), where grief support lets people know they are not alone. Here they are a part of a caring and loving community. They work through their grief to a place of healing and can draw on the experiences and encouragement of friends and fellow grievers.

The grief support group aids in the attendees' healing. It helps them move on and find continued meaning in life. Their participation will bring comfort and understanding beyond their expectations. "A Safe Place" allows them to grow through grief, feeling accepted, loved, and understood, but mostly to let them know that God is in the business of healing. How particularly important they are to Him.

It is important to celebrate the life of those we have lost, just as it is important to continue celebrating the family members who are moving forward. ASP has established Candlelight Services to celebrate both.

What was so comforting in the creation of this piece was that I also needed healing. Every time I visited research on death and dying, I became stronger. I found this to be the balm for my pain.

As I continued this journey of discovery, I became stronger in who I am and not who I was. I was convinced that I was created to be a vessel chosen by God. I was created to carry the torch of His Light into darkness. I was chosen to be His agent of change!

Another class that got my attention was Christian Education. This is where we were asked to write about a ministry we would like to begin or work with. I wrote the educational plan for the Delores Foundation. I remember my professor asking me to let her know the start date of this ministry, and I did.

The Lord directed me to the cemetery where my family was buried, and I could not understand why. I viewed the headstones of family members and began to write down each person's birth and death dates. I looked a short distance away and saw the headstone of a close friend of our family.

I noticed that the birth date of the gentleman was the same as my son's. I froze at once. You see, a few years ago, I found out that there was a strong possibility that this gentleman could have been my biological father. I had lived with the pain for so many years of just wanting to know who my father was. Nobody would tell me, and I could not understand why. I still don't know for sure.

I began reading all the other headstones of people I remembered from childhood. I recalled that most of them had drinking problems. For years, I heard they were alcoholics, which is what they died from. But God revealed to me that day that they had died from a broken heart. He also informed me why he had delivered me from a life of personal destruction. God needed me.

Oh yes, I have been through the fire and through the flood, but I am still here, in Jesus' name. I give God all the Praise. I am a willing vessel to do His will.

"I will praise You, for I am fearfully and wonderfully made; Marvelous are Your works, and that my soul knows very well." - Psalm 139:14 (NKJV)

I now know beyond doubt that God has chosen me to spread His word, that He is the Lord of Lords, the Alpha, and the Omega. He sits high and looks low and loves us all. He forgives us of our sins, and all we need to do is acknowledge Him as our Lord and our Savior.

"Now to Him who is able to do exceedingly abundantly above all that we ask or think, according to the power that works in us." - Ephesians 3:20 (NKJV)

After acknowledging my call to ministry and gaining the training from my pastor, it was time for me to deliver my initial sermon. There was a lady who was a member of my church by the name of Jeanette Woodson. I looked for her sweet, smiling face every Sunday I had to sing. Her presence gave me peace. She became extremely ill and was absent from church, but her spirit was always with me.

I visited her when I received the green light to preach. By then, she was bedridden. I was so excited about the good news regarding the beginning of preaching that I found myself lying in bed beside her, but when I told her, she said, "I already know." WOW! How news spreads. She told me how she had been praying for me and that everything would be all right.

While struggling through the sermon preparation, all I had to do was think of her. After I had preached, I headed straight to her home to share the good news; by then, she was transitioning from her earthly dwelling to receive her reward. I kissed her on the forehead, thanked her, and told her that I loved her. I was licensed to preach in March of 2006.

Even though I did not march to receive my high school diploma or business school diploma, God opened the door for me to march for the first time to receive my Master of Theology on May 9, 2007. I cried most of that day because this was the anniversary of Mommy's funeral. I know she would have been proud.

I became a student at Virginia Commonwealth University's program in Patient Counseling in 2008. This is where I acquired Clinical Pastoral Education.

When I began my journey as a chaplain, I was terrified and refused to turn my pager on, but one Friday night, I said to myself, I am not going to walk in fear. As soon as I turned it on, a call came, and I went to the emergency room. They had just brought in a gentleman who was found dead in his field.

My job was to comfort his wife. She was so distraught; all she wanted to do was see him. I wheeled her to the examining room, and that was the longest trip ever. I had to help her out of the wheelchair to view him. I did not sleep for nights after that visit.

There was a learning contract that I developed consisting of several goals. My first goal was to advance my reflective/active listening skills. I believe that I have worked earnestly to achieve this goal. Working towards this goal allowed me the opportunity to be more attentive to conversations between patients, as well as conversations with their families.

I was able to engage in active listening by learning how not to allow my mind to wander into my past as I listened to the stories shared. I was able to give my undivided attention as I listened.

My second goal was not to allow myself to lose sight of the compassionate spirit given to me by God. Working toward achieving this goal was quite monumental. I never wanted to build a wall of protection to guard my emotions when visiting a patient.

It was not hard for me to continue having a compassionate spirit. The visits, especially to the ER department, became extremely overwhelming. When I looked back on pain of my past, I could draw from my experiences and used God's deliverance to speak to me as I ministered.

Prayer was the key. I prayed for God to walk before each visit, and if the visit became very intense, then I was able to download prayers and music, which was very therapeutic. I would retreat to the office and conduct my own praise service. I am very thankful to God for who I am and for what He has called me to do.

My third goal was to reach a comfortable level in the prayers I offer on behalf of those with whom I paid a visit. WOW! This goal was truly major for me because I know the seriousness of prayer. It was never my desire to utter a prayer that would cause any damage to the patient or the family. I had been given a window of opportunity to speak a word of encouragement through prayer. To work through this goal, I had to engage in intercessory prayer for patients. This strengthened me tremendously.

I viewed myself as a needed presence in the hospital setting. I witnessed the calmness that came over the staff when I visited them. My heart was touched many times when a nurse would hug me. It told me that I mattered because I showed them how valuable they were.

Sometimes, I wondered if God wanted me to participate in this program. There were times when I could not see the forest for the trees. There were so many obstacles that were in my way.

I asked God if I heard Him or was it my own voice that I was following. Why was I giving up on myself when God had not? I cried and prayed, prayed and cried, but God's loving hand kept me and guided me on my way. This was a faith walk, and God gave me the strength I needed. God met me in my brokenness and carried me. When I wanted to stop this program, I could not. I knew that God was still God and that I had to trust Him and continue.

My friend, confidante, and intercessor, Bessie Smith, received many calls from me, especially after tending to a patient and their family. She would talk to me while traveling from Petersburg, VA, to Glen Allen, VA. God would always send us what we need.

I believe the many losses in my life have shaped me for the ministry of Pastoral Care. I said this because there have been people who have experienced the same losses and did not make it. God has allowed me to live, and it is because He had a plan for my life.

I have been engaged in a variety of relationships. Some of them have been painful, and some have been most rewarding. Some have been short-lived, and then some have been for a lifetime. I have learned from my relationships to appreciate all the good and ask God to show me the other side of what was not so good. He has taught me the value of relationships and to know that each one serves a purpose.

I became extremely excited about listening to people from other social classes share their stories. Their lifestyles intrigue me, and this is because of my desire to understand people and their cultures. America is all I know, and when I meet people of other races, it is an international journey for me.

God loves all people, and as an agent of God, I too must love all people. This is a prerequisite for ministry. I also believe that we who God calls cannot truly minister until we can love all people from all levels of society. This

Clinical Pastoral Educational journey allowed me to minister to people from all social classes. All I saw was a child of God when I was in their presence.

As I was becoming groomed in the ministry of Pastoral Care, I began to understand the connection. God has called me to minister to many, and many means anybody, whether they look like me or not.

Even though I wholeheartedly believe that I have earnestly worked to meet each goal, I would continue to strengthen my goals through visits with congregants, as well as to use the resources provided through this program. I graduated in December 2009 with a Patient Counseling Certificate, and I will continue the educational journey as the world changes. This was a program that significantly changed my life as I matriculated through it and became a chaplain.

"I waited patiently for the Lord to help me, and he turned to me and heard my cry." - Psalm 40:1 (NLT)

Chapter 10

Higher Ground

In 2012, I felt led to apply to Virginia Union School of Theology and pursue my Doctor of Ministry degree. I solicited help from one of the professors and completed the admissions process. I waited and waited and waited but heard nothing. When I contacted him, I was informed I was not accepted. Of course, I was crushed, and until this day, I am still waiting for my rejection letter. This was a testimony to "Delayed but Not Denied."

Oh yes, God was in the middle and was working it all out for my good. One day while cleaning my bedroom, I saw this beautiful logo and the mention of Capella University. I knew about the school through a dear friend, Gabriella Caldwell-Miller, who was a graduate.

I halted - stopped watching and listening to the commercial. I was dumbfounded but did not know why. I sat down on the side of the bed and soaked in the information. I asked God, is this where He desired me to attend? Over a period, the peace of His presence was my green light.

I contacted my dear friend, Gabby, and informed her of my application. I got in touch with one of the advisors, who provided all the information needed for the application process. I had been informed by a close friend that I would not be accepted because I had not earned a bachelor's degree, but I moved forward anyway. I informed the advisor that I was interested in applying for the Master of Science degree with a concentration in Mental Health.

I am so grateful to God that I heard His call and followed through with my education. Whenever I thought about going back to school at the age of sixty-two, I felt that was a hindrance. I quickly dismissed that notion because God knew my age which is not at all an issue with him.

When the advisor asked about my previous educational journey, he could not understand how I earned a master's without a bachelor's. I did not comment, and then he stated, "As long as you have a master's degree."

When you know that God is prompting you to move forward, you cannot listen to naysayers. You must lean, depend on and trust God because His word is true, and He will direct your steps.

In January of 2012, I began my educational journey through Capella University, and it was a powerful journey. This was also a process of healing for me because I saw myself in so many scenarios. I gained an understanding of mommy's pain. She lived with major depression. The studying and the writing were over the top, but I was determined to press on and press through. "I can do all things through Christ who strengthens me." - Philippians 4:13 (NKJV)

With the aid of the Holy Spirit and the blessing of my family and dear friends, I gained what I needed for so many years. I saw God's healing hands over me, and I felt His presence with every class taken. When I began earning "A's," it felt like I was someone else, but no, this was Vanessa who had earned those "A's." When I earned a "B," I was devastated but eventually got over it.

I have a friend, Karen McAdoo, who always encouraged me with, "You've Got This." I have another friend, Brenda Encarnacion, who would always say, "Stay Focused." One of them, however, did not want to hear how I acquired an "A" because she stated that it was not a surprise.

They did not know how horrible of a student I was throughout my middle, high school, and business school years. Reflecting on those years, I am now clear on how deep my depression was. Achieving what would have been good was not on my radar. But God!

There were courses that gave me more understanding of what I had experienced in life. Those were very painful experiences, and they left scars. I was amazed at how my studies touched me in so many ways.

The last leg of the journey led me to have the opportunity of entering an internship with a private practice. Little did I know after meeting the owner during my first year of school, I would be led to ask her to become my internship supervisor. We had developed a dual relationship. She also became my friend (April St. John).

I did not want to receive my degree in the mail. I wanted to march across that stage and receive it in my hand, so we went to Minneapolis, Minnesota. My husband, Michael, Godmother Doris, and grandson Angel traveled with me. On September 13, 2016, by the grace of God, I received my Master of Science in Mental Health Counseling.

After graduation, I became a Resident Counselor at Living Anew Counseling and was able to continue under April St. John's leadership. I was also able to keep the clients I counseled while in school as well as gain more.

During counseling sessions, I heard my own story, and there were times I had to widen my eyes in order not to shed tears. It was about the clients and not about me. What I found out was that my compassion heightened as I sat with my clients.

I am so grateful for the opportunity to minister as a Pastoral Counselor with Barnabas Counseling Ministry, as well as a former leader of the Grief Support Group at my church (St. Paul's Baptist Church). This ministry had already been established, and God allowed me to walk through the doors and spread His healing touch to the hurting.

I am now a Resident Counselor with Packlight Counseling, LLC, a dream job, and I am so grateful to God for opening this absolutely impressive door. He continues to allow me to walk through valleys with my clients to help bring them to a place of healing and peace in their lives.

When I reflect on this journey, I am so incredibly grateful. When the road becomes bumpy, I am reminded of who called me on this journey. Then I am refreshed and continue to move in the direction God has ordained.

"Make you complete in every good work to do His will, working in you what is well pleasing in His sight, through Jesus Christ, to whom be glory forever and ever. Amen."
– Hebrews 13:21 (NKJV)

Chapter 11

Totally Available

My beginning was God knitting me in my mother's womb and choosing the day I would enter this world. He had already planted seeds that would take root in their season. God's hand has been in my life from the very beginning, knowing what I would encounter. As those challenging times surfaced, His angels were even closer to protect me.

The desire to become a pianist led me to learn some of the most uplifting hymns that began to feed my spirit at an early age. Hymns such as "Lead Me, Guide Me," "Oh Thou Great Jehovah," Oh the Blood of Jesus," "Nothing but the Blood," "Holy, Holy, Holy," "Great is thy Faithfulness," and "He Kept Me in The Midst of It All." These are just a few that followed me through my life and continue to fuel my soul.

My daydreaming in elementary school was the start of becoming a visionary which would come to fruition years later. It gave life to The Delores Foundation and Your Extended Support Services. Those planted seeds began to shed their outer shells and are growing. I believe there are seeds that have still not sprouted, and that gives me hope.

I am now living my best life as God had already ordained. He has given me the right to counsel, dedicate, lead, officiate, pray, preach, and teach. I now know who I am – I am a child of the Highest God, who was created to be His earthly vessel to shower love on those around me.

Visiting me this past summer were butterflies. Each represented those who have gone on to be with the Lord. My birth mother, my mommy, my daddy, my son, my grandmother, and my great-grandmother. The butterflies' visits brought a smile to my face and a sense of peace. It was God's way of letting me know that they were watching over me.

This past year I was blessed with an opportunity to present a play titled "Meet Me in the Garden" at the neighborhood church where I was raised. I had not been to Washington Park in 48 years, so the visit brought memories. Instead of tears, I smiled as I walked the streets. Even though time has changed the landscape of homes, many remain just as I remembered. Thank You, God!

I am at peace because I don't know who my biological father is, but thanks to Daddy Lorenza, who was my father figure, and to God, my heavenly father. If God desires for me to know, He will make it happen.

I forgave mommy and daddy for the pain they inflicted. I forgave the men who violated me. I have asked God's forgiveness for any pain I have caused others. I have forgiven myself and walk in freedom each day.

"And whenever you stand praying, if you have anything against anyone, forgive him, that your Father in heaven may also forgive you your trespasses. But if you do not forgive, neither will your Father in heaven forgive your trespasses."- Marks 11:25-26(NKJV).

God knew all along why He created me the way He did. It is for such a time as now. For so often, I have felt different, an outsider, and did not fit in. I thought I was abnormal, but I now live under what God's definition of being "NORMAL" really is.

Oh, sure, I have my moments, but during those times, I drew closer to God. I believe that is why those days came. God wanted my undivided attention. He has something He needs to share with me; therefore, I need to be available.

When I look back over my life and think things over, I can honestly say I have been blessed. I have a testimony. If I had not lived the life I lived, I would not be who I am today, Vanessa Patricia Bowers Carter. "I Am the Face of Hope!" I Made It to Tell the Story.

"Now to Him who is able to do exceedingly abundantly above all that we ask or think, according to the power that works in us, to Him be glory in the church by Christ Jesus to all generations, forever and ever. Amen." - Ephesians 3:20-21(NKJV)

About The Author

Rev. Vanessa B. Carter is a woman of God who has committed her life to serving the wounded. She is a compassionate soul who has a listening ear, a word of encouragement and a hug. She is the founder and CEO of "The Delores Foundation, Inc." whose mission is to provide transitional services and resources to girls and single women with children, empowering them to achieve physical, mental, and emotional stability.

Vanessa is also the CEO of Your Extended Support Services whose mission is to provide grief support and training in the community. Vanessa is also a Pastoral Counselor at St. Paul's Baptist Church in Richmond, VA. She is a pre-licensed Counselor with Packlight Counseling, LLC in Mechanicsville, VA.

Vanessa is enthusiastic in the areas of being an accomplished gardener, musician, and singer. God has blessed her with a loving husband (Michael), a son (Mikey) and grandson (Angel). With their support, she is fulfilling what God has ordained for her life.

She is a prayerful and powerful woman of God, whom she seeks daily. She knows His love and how it can help others heal, and she shares His love and joy wherever she goes. This is the charge Rev. Carter has placed upon herself and one she lives every day to see fulfilled. Whoever God allows to cross her path with a need, her desire is to be a vessel of healing and hope.

"The Spirit of the Lord is upon me, because he has anointed me to proclaim good news to the poor. He has sent me to proclaim liberty to the captives and recovering of sight to the blind, to set at liberty those who are oppressed, to proclaim the year of the Lord's favor." - Luke 4:18, 19 (ESV)

Made in the USA
Columbia, SC
10 October 2022